Wonder Walking:
Enjoying the Wonders
of Walking Outdoors

Terilee Wunderman

Terilee Wunderman
Formatted: English (United States)
Wunderman & Wunderman, P.A.
8600 S.W. 92 Street, Suite 203
Miami, Florida 33156
www.DrWunderman.com

ISBN-13: 978-1548110505
ISBN-10: 1548110507

Miami, Florida/Terilee Wunderman – Second Edition

All the photos in this book were taken by Terilee Wunderman.

An Invitation to the Reader

In the photograph on the previous page, you'll notice a lighted path with a protective canopy of delicate, lush greenery. This image symbolizes the natural light present always. It also symbolizes growth along our journey and the soothing beauty of nature that's always available.

At the same time, the image includes the human-made pavement that provides a solid foundation along with a metal box housing phone cables, necessary interruptions in nature that allow us to communicate and connect with one another. Instead of allowing those images to take away or diminish the beauty of the light-filled path ahead, Wonder Walking allows us to include them as simply part of our experience, and at times blessings, along the way. By tuning into the wonder of all things, we can find new ways to perceive what might have felt bothersome or annoying. We can see the value in all that is present by allowing the light to shine and reveal the goodness in all.

Wonder Walking:
Enjoying the Wonders
of Walking Outdoors

This book is intended as a friendly, supportive guide
for enjoying walking outdoors.
If at any time you have concerns about your
physical, mental, emotional or spiritual well-being,
please consult a professional for support and guidance.

All things in this creation exist within you,
and all things in you exist in creation;
there is no border
between you and the closest things,
and there is no distance
between you and the farthest things,
and all things,
from the lowest to the loftiest,
from the smallest to the greatest,
are within you as equal things.

Kahlil Gibran

Florida Knight Anole

Table of Contents

> *I believe a leaf of grass is no less*
> *than the journey-work of the stars.*
>
> *Walt Whitman*

Young Tree Frog
Resting in a Shrub

Why Wonder Walk?

Are you someone who is interested in learning more about experiencing a sense of wonder as you walk? Would you like to feel a sense of oneness with all that surrounds you? Even for just a moment?

Do you ever find yourself thinking, "I need to wind down, but I really need to get inspired, but I also need some exercise?"

These three thoughts can seem contradictory, but Wonder Walking blends them together.

When you Wonder Walk, you allow your surroundings to nurture you as you move and breathe. You can clear your mind of worries and concerns as you tune into the wonder and oneness of all around you. You can experience openness to the natural inspiration that walking outdoors provides.

Bougainvillea Beauty

Wonder Walking is a delightful approach to easy exercise and personal renewal. It combines gentle self-care infused with the blessings of the oneness and wonder of all things present. Wonder Walking is about walking as you choose to walk, in ways that are comfortable for you, while noticing and enjoying the simple yet wondrous sights and sounds along your path.

I wrote this book because I love walking outdoors. Tuning into the oneness of my surroundings soothes and inspires me as well as helps me relax and clear my mind while getting helpful exercise. By walking in appreciation for the wonder of my surroundings, I've learned to find the blessings in each experience along my way. It's a wonderful way to approach walking through life!

Arika Palm Frond Peeking Through

In this book, you will explore and experience the wonder and oneness in all that is present while simply walking outdoors.

Imagine exploring:

How nature nurtures you
Greater acceptance of all
    things
Improving your health
Clearing your mind
Freeing emotions
Renewed sense about life
Ordinary miracles of
    nature
Awe of natural life cycles
Rejuvenation

If you are ready to take better care of yourself and enjoy more of the wonder around you, welcome to Wonder Walking. Welcome to easy, peaceful ways to move your body while enjoying the blessings and gentle nurturance of your surroundings.

*A human being is part of the whole
called by us universe,
a part limited in time and space.
We experience ourselves,
our thoughts and feelings
as something separate from the rest,
a kind of optical delusion of consciousness.*

*This delusion is a kind of prison for us,
restricting us to our personal desires
and to affection for a few persons
nearest to us.*

*Our task must be to free ourselves
from the prison
by widening our circle of compassion
to embrace all living creatures
and the whole of nature in its beauty.*

Albert Einstein

*Staghorn Fern on a
Gumbo Limbo Tree*

Is Wonder Walking for You?

Wonder Walking is for people who would like to:

~Enhance the natural healing properties of walking
~Experience a sense of oneness with all things
~Increase awareness of blessings already present

*Peace and Calm on
an Often Busy Street*

At first glance, combining self-care and walking outdoors might sound like just another approach to exercise. It might seem like an impossible combination to truly take care of oneself while moving and sweating amidst the noise and bustle of cars, trucks and lawn mowers. You might think you would need to be too alert and vigilant, trying to avoid the noise and interference, in order to be able to clear your mind in any manner.

Maybe you say to yourself, "I already know how to walk. The outdoors is the same as always. What would be different?"

Perhaps you doubt that this approach would offer anything new, different or better for you. Experiencing a sense of wonder might seem elusive or non-existent. In fact, it might sound ridiculous to even consider there are blessings present while walking near loud, smelly traffic or noisy construction equipment, amidst smog or humidity, or around barking dogs, slimy earthworms, or piles of trash.

Yet, if you simply ask yourself, "What's the good here? How could this experience be a blessing?" you open yourself to the wonder of it all. You can allow yourself to experience the oneness of the divine, however you conceptualize the One that created everything --- from diesel fumes to fragrant roses.

When we walk outdoors, we are able to tune in to how nature is supporting us naturally and in harmony. We breathe with regularity and rhythm. Sounds from outdoors can harmonize with us even when those noises are human-made.

Sunset Reflections

We can tune into the rhythms of motors, the cycling of revolving engines, or the hums, whirs and groans of turbines. We can appreciate how each sound plays a part in the harmonizing of our existence – whether it's chirping, croaking, scampering, buzzing, drilling or grinding. All sounds are in some way reflecting how we as a species are caring for ourselves.

Gardeners tend to our yards and the swales between sidewalks and roadways. Garbage trucks clean up our neighborhoods, caring for us with their grand engines, loud mechanisms and noisy, grinding movements. Vehicles transport us with occasional honks to warn us and keep things moving. How we choose to perceive these noises has everything to do with how we allow ourselves to experience the harmony and basic goodness of all that goes on around us. We can choose to appreciate the ways these interruptions and distractions actually serve us and our communities.

When you Wonder Walk, you notice how your body connects with the earth, air and surroundings. Your feet align with the pavement, grass and dirt, adjusting naturally to cracks in the sidewalk, rocks and pebbles, inclines and slopes, soft ground, muddy patches and even puddles. You avoid lizards scurrying in front of you as well as snails and worms that inch along, often surfacing on sidewalks after rain showers flooded their underground homes. Your eyes notice these things, and your feet, ankles and legs adjust automatically, often without your conscious awareness or at least for not more than a moment.

*Mowing the Grass
in Early Morning Light*

Your arms swing in complementary, synchronous movements with your legs. You may feel a breeze on your sweaty skin, cooling you naturally. The wind may gust, making your clothes rustle and your hair fly up and sideways. Your breathing may become easier or perhaps more effortful as the air changes around you. You adjust to the rhythms of weather and nature, in harmony and with a sense of natural synchronicity.

You may touch a leaf, smell a flower, or pick up a branch or interesting pebble. Maybe you find a lucky penny or even a dollar bill. Perhaps you pick up an empty can or paper bag, a bottle cap, candy wrapper or cigarette butt, helping to care for your surroundings.

By walking with a sense of cooperation for what you encounter, you can allow yourself to experience the oneness with all things. By noticing what surrounds you, from the smallest leaf to the grandest tree, you can increase your awareness of the infinite blessings already present. From this openness and appreciation for the goodness all around, you invite yourself into an experience of greater health and well-being.

Gentle Fog Softens
an Early Morning View

Heavenly Wild Flower

Tips for Wonder Walking

Suggestions

Wear comfortable clothing and sneakers
Wear a hat or visor
Dress for the weather
Use insect repellent and sunscreen
Choose a safe area
Pay attention
Listen inwardly and outwardly
Be open to gratitude
Breath naturally
Keep moving

Sunset towards the Everglades

Blessings of Service Workers

What to Avoid

Expecting quiet
Walking too fast
Walking for too long
Dismissing things as irrelevant
Phone calling/emailing/texting
Expecting quick fitness or rapid weight loss
Looking down all the time
Keeping arms still
Judging experiences
Worrying

Wonder & Awe

Privacy of thoughts and feelings
Freedom of thoughts and feelings
Pleasure in walking alone
Pleasure in walking with others
Better breathing
Communing with nature
Harmonizing with noises
Connection to others
Being of service
Inner peace and calm

Storm Rolling in at Sunset

Cuddling Ducks

My Story of Wonder Walking

My history experiencing the wonder of nature begins back
when I was small and enjoyed treasured time alone in my
backyard. I spotted tiny plum-colored flowers with
delicate white petals on low lying weeds. I found
miniature white daisies with bright golden centers. The
small miracles fit comfortably and perfectly in my young
hands. They were precious flowers to me, not weeds to be
discarded. I honored them as bouquets and hair wreaths
for my dolls.

I found solace and
comfort sitting under a
grand Ficus tree, leaning
against its sturdy trunk
or swinging on a branch
that fit into my tiny young
hands. I explored the way
our thin metal fence
disappeared mysteriously
into the sandy earth
below. As I grew tall
enough, I reached over that fence and hugged a tall dark
brown tree trunk that served as a stately electrical pole,
one that never teetered even through numerous
hurricanes.

In our yard, I found snails that suctioned themselves to
windows, clotheslines and swings. I watched lime green
lizards scurry away as soon as I neared them, and I
learned over time how to approach them carefully and
quietly so I could watch them up close. I sat on our front
step as dark brown slugs slithered slowly across our front
sidewalk, leaving a shiny line trailing behind them,
oblivious to my presence.

I marveled at the differences in the ways things lived and how they cooperated in harmony with one another. Plants served as homes for butterflies, bees and ladybugs. Trees served as homes for birds and even for woodpeckers who made holes in their trunks.

Puddles from rain showers became breeding grounds for mosquitos that pierced my skin before I sensed their delicate black legs settling on me. Ripe coconuts landed on the ground beneath tall palm trees, providing us with refreshing coconut milk and chunks of yummy treats right in our front yard. With oranges and mangoes within my arm's reach, I savored a delicious array of nature's gifts just by stepping outdoors.

When I was a bit older, my interest in walking outdoors grew as I began realizing that walking outdoors by myself helped me not only feel physically better but also clearer in my mind and my heart. I had turned seventeen and was attending the local community college while living at home with my parents. Most of my friends had left to attend universities out of town. I missed my friends and found that the main way to recharge myself after work and school, as well as to have space from my parents, was when I took a walk by myself. After each walk, I felt renewed energy to face whatever challenges I had in front of me.

Most early evenings, I walked our two dachshunds around the block where I lived in our quiet, suburban neighborhood. I found myself noticing things outdoors as I had when I was younger. I looked at the different ways people landscaped their yards and how cats and squirrels scurried away as they heard us nearing.

In my head, I sorted out things that happened during the day, what I was trying to understand, as well as fantasies and dreams I held for when I would finish community college and leave home. The walking and inner-talking helped me relax my mind while relieving my body of stress and tension from the day. I felt my loneliness diminish as I connected to what went on around me --- a gentle breeze on my arms, the soft crunch of leaves under my sneakers, birds chirping above me as they flew in perfect Vs, cats meowing from behind bushes --- all in wondrous harmony with each other as well as me.

Sometimes I went jogging, but running didn't have the same nurturing, soothing effects on me as paced walking. Running wasn't meditative or comforting in the way focused, clarifying walking was for me. When I ran, I didn't get to enjoy what I

saw to the depth I did when I walked. I missed the awe and wonder of the beauty around me as I instead focused on keeping my pace, enduring and needing quicker reflexes. The steady, comfortable and less vigilant pace of walking suited me better. So I quickened my pace while keeping my sneakers on the ground.

Pacing myself across pavement, grass and leaves while listening to the humming and buzzing of insects around me, I felt connected and soothed by the synchronicity and oneness of all things. My breathing eased into a deep, hearty and rhythmic inhale and exhale. My mind cleared as my worries and concerns dissolved and faded away. I returned from my walks spent but renewed. Tired but refreshed. Filled with grace over the ease of my exercise --- a miraculous combination of healthy exhaustion and welcome rejuvenation.

One day some years later, my sister leant me a portable cassette player and encouraged me to listen to music while I walked. As a long-distance runner, she found the player essential for her endurance as well as being a profound enhancer for her running experience. Although carrying the player felt awkward at first, I quickly found myself forgetting about the small machine in my hand and instead became at one with the beauty of the sounds in my ears.

Tree Canopy

I listened to the cassette she had in the player --- *Beethoven's Sixth Symphony*. When I first heard the symphony through my earbuds, amidst the canopy of trees covering my path, my heart swelled with the inner and outer beauty occurring simultaneously. I found myself blending the sounds of traffic, lawn mowers and construction machinery with the harmonizing of the strings and horns. I could hear the oneness of the rhythms and beats, the sounds of humanity expressing itself in its many different forms. My eyes filled with tears as I tuned into the awesome synchronicity of the divine music and the ordinariness of the busy world around me.

A journey of a thousand miles begins with a single step.

Lao Tzu

Walking and Self-Care

Self-care is one of the best ways to experience your divinity and the divinity of all around you. When you take care of yourself, you are honoring the divine source within that breathes you alive in each moment. You are allowing the divine to fortify you so you can go out into the world ready and able to meet the challenges ahead and open to doing good works.

As you care for yourself, you demonstrate that you love who you are. That love grows within you and can extend out to others naturally.

Caring for ourselves has to suit each of us individually. If we try to take care of ourselves in ways that are uncomfortable or too much of stretch for us, then we aren't likely to keep at it. We'll avoid it, thinking we're being bad, wrong or incompetent.

*Potted Palm
in Morning Sun*

In truth, we just need to find more suitable ways to nurture who we are --- physically, emotionally, mentally and spiritually --- ways that work for us individually.

Caring for oneself is deeply personal, profoundly private, and yet connected to everything around us. We are never alone. We are always in some way connected, affected and interacting with our surroundings.

Caring for ourselves is also a 24/7 practice. Self-care matters throughout the day as well as when we are asleep. It involves our awareness and attention to what truly helps us in all kinds of ways and all the time.

Self-care can involve allowing the oneness, the grace and blessings in all things, to come into our awareness. We can make a choice for where we focus ourselves. We can choose to see the goodness in all things regardless of what we may first perceive or judge about what we observe or hear.

The value of caring for oneself is the foundation of my life and my work helping others. The first step to be of help to anyone involves self-care, and self-care begins with our

My Neighbor's Orchid

divine creator, however you conceptualize the source of your being. Tuning into that loving creative source within - which I believe is within everyone and everything - encourages me to know it further and in greater ways. I am then moved to support others to know the value of self-care as the foundation for greater health and well-being as well as creativity and productivity.

I've seen time and again how taking care of ourselves first provides the fuel and foundation for all healing and growth. The more we connect with the oneness and grace present within us and around us, the better for all. The more we seek and find the blessings and all the goodness that is here for us, the better we will feel and function by ourselves and with others.

Wonder Walking is not the only way or the best way for everyone to care for themselves. There are infinitely different ways, just as there are infinitely different people in the world. However, Wonder Walking is one way that can work for some people as it has for me.

I welcome you.

Morning Sun
on my Front Doorstep

*The walking of which I speak
has nothing in it akin to taking exercise,
as it is called,
as the sick take medicine at stated hours
. . . but it is itself the enterprise
and adventure of the day.*

Henry David Thoreau

Walking and Health

While any natural movement can improve our physical health, walking helps in key gentle ways. When we walk uphill or downhill or on a variety of textures such as grass, gravel, pavement and sand, we use our muscles in different ways. We stress our joints more and strengthen muscle fibers that we might not otherwise (Vindum, 2009)

Vindum found that, "When we move our bodies and get our heart pumping and circulation going, our brain feeds on oxygen. We need it for energy—it is literally food for the brain and muscles."

Foundational Roots

When we walk outdoors, we breathe fresh air which is usually healthier for us. Some indoor pollution rates have been found to be higher than outdoor rates, as much as fifty times higher (U.S. EPA).

Spending time in nature "helps rest a part of the brain that's involved in mental effort," notes Frances Kuo, Ph.D. in Vindum's report. By being outdoors and connecting to our environment, we give our mind a chance to recuperate from indoor stress. After a walk, we are more ready and able to face the challenges awaiting us when we return indoors.

Researchers at the National Institute of Mental Health found that compared with walking indoors on a treadmill, people found walking in natural environments to be more revitalizing and helpful for experiencing a positive relationship to the environment. After a simple stroll outside, people reported less tension, fatigue and depression while at the same time they experienced more vitality, enthusiasm, pleasure and self-esteem. The NIMH researchers also learned that people who walked outdoors found greater enjoyment and satisfaction with the actual experience of outdoor walking than those who had the experience of walking on a treadmill or around an indoor track (Thompson et al, 2011).

View from Standing
"Inside" a Tree

In a study from the United Kingdom, a walk outdoors at lunch time helped people sleep better the following night. The lunchtime walkers also woke up feeling more restored the next day compared to mornings when they hadn't walked outdoors the day before. When people walked regularly outdoors, they had significantly lower blood pressure. In addition, after just eight weeks of walking outdoors several days a week, walkers felt much less stress in their lives. With as little as five minutes of outdoor exercise, people felt significant boosts in mood and self-esteem, including those who suffered with diagnosed mental disorders (Nichols & Watts, 2014).

New Growth on an Aged Root

Spending time outdoors can make a significant improvement in your psychological well-being, even you live in an urban environment. Researchers found that people who spent time in green environments, even if those environments existed within an urban area, felt better emotionally, had improved attention, and experienced less stress and anxiety in their daily lives. In deprived urban communities where green environments were minimal but still available, researchers found that people who spent time in those green areas had improved cognitive abilities as well as a greater sense of self-discipline. At the same time, those challenged communities reported reduced aggression and lowered crime rates in the areas where green environments were incorporated into the urban setting. (Thompson et al, 2012).

The action of walking, and its accompanying cardio-respiratory benefits, appears strongly related to memory enhancement. Neuroscience researchers found that taking a brisk walk helped people improve their memory. In this study, adults were asked questions about something told to them a day earlier. The researchers found that people who took a brisk walk remembered the information they learned better than those who were simply asked questions without having the chance to take a walk, either outdoors or on a treadmill (Span, 2011).

The value of walking outdoors has been found repeatedly in research studies regardless of the actual location. Psychology researchers found that students who viewed photos of nature shortly after being exposed to a stressful task reported increased feelings of affection, playfulness, friendliness and elation. However, students who viewed photos of urban scenes after the same stressful tasks reported feeling increased sadness (Nichols & Watts, 2014).

Studies from the Japanese Society of Forest Medicine (2010) found that people who took walks in the forest had lowered cortisol levels compared with people who walked the same distance indoors in a lab environment. The studies also showed that walking in the forests had long-lasting positive effects on the immune system. Certain natural chemicals released by trees travel through

Morning Light in Fog

the air and are linked to our improved immune defenses, reduced anxiety, and increased pain thresholds.

Walk as if you are kissing the earth with your feet.

Thich Nhat Hanh

Walking and Spirituality

Often when we think of tuning into the divine, we tend to focus on stillness through meditation, prayer, yoga, massage, or time in a spa or hot tub.   While sitting still or lying down is good for certain types of meditative practices, moving is another way to tune into our divinity and the ever-flowing natural energy of the divine. Through Wonder Walking, we can have the experience of our body and environment being divinely and joyfully connected in movement.

The essence of our spirit is never actually still. Even in the quiet, our spiritual source is flowing, moving and expanding, keeping us breathing and our hearts beating. When we sit or kneel in prayer, we make our bodies still so we can focus on our thoughts, higher power and inner wisdom. Sometimes we need to be still in order to allow that inner spirit to come through, to hear

Angelic Cloud Formation at Sunset

those inner words and messages of guidance and solace. Other times, it is through movement that we tune into the divine energy flow. Wonder Walking as a self-care practice puts us in harmonious synchronicity with nature's wonder and the eternal movement of the spirit.

Walking outdoors as a healing, self-care practice can be done at any age. Whether we walk unassisted or we use a cane or a walker, we can move at a pace that is comfortable and healing for us. Walking through the different ages of our lives helps us be aware of the many ages of whatever we see outdoors.

Divine Canopy

Plants move through various stages of growth above, beside and beneath us. Flowers appear in buds, luscious blooms, or withered remains. Grass may be neatly mowed and trimmed or overgrown and weedy. Branches may reach out and upward, filled with leaves, or they may be barren, broken or fallen to the ground.

Sidewalks may be clean and smooth or marked with holes and scattered with dirt. Potholes may dot the streets while newly-paved roads shine with fresh surfaces. Houses may have new siding or paint or be under construction while others may show the signs of weather-beaten wear and tear.

We can walk by ourselves or with someone by our side, maybe hand-in-hand. We can push a loved one in a stroller or a wheelchair. We can walk with a dog or the occasional cat. We can walk, sit and rest, walk some more, stroll slowly or move at a brisk pace.

We can carry an umbrella to avoid a shower or shade us from the bright sun. We can protect ourselves with a hat or visor, use insect repellent, and wear loose, breezy clothing. Other times, we wear warm sweatshirts with snuggly hoods, fleece pants, and insulated socks. All are ways we sense and observe ourselves in connection with our surroundings as we walk in wonder, with appreciation and in cooperation with all.

An Occasional Cat
Sharing a Wonder Walk

After a Fresh Shower

Walking and Creativity

People are often more creative when they are actually walking than when they are sitting still. While taking a brief walk, students at Stanford University gave more creative responses to simple questions than those who were sitting still when asked the same questions. Even a brief stroll helped people tap into their natural creativity and increase their creative expression. Upon returning from a brief walk, many subjects found their creativity still easy to access and express even when they sat down and were still, suggesting a walk has long-lasting positive effects on creativity (Oppezzo & Schwartz, 2014).

Royal Poinciana

Nature's Fireworks

In a study at the University of Surrey in England, walking was found to improve the ability to shift between modes of thought by encouraging flexible thinking processes. Walking helped improve attention and memory as well as recovery from mental fatigue, all key factors for creative thinking. By being exposed to the constant flux of changes around us, especially when we venture outdoors, we are provided new and ever-changing experiences to which we can react and learn.

While walking, we refer naturally to our past experiences and memories as we observe and take in new sights, sounds and experiences. Our new awarenesses can provoke new associations, meanings and insights about the past while promoting the birth of new ideas.

Some of the great musical composers relied on daily walks outdoors to find inspiration to create their works. Tchaikovsky, Mahler and Beethoven all took paper and pencil with them on their daily walks which often occurred shortly after lunch. During their strolls, they stopped briefly to jot down ideas and musical thoughts that came to them. When they returned home, they would then incorporate their inspirations into great musical works (Currey, 2013).

All truly great thoughts are conceived by walking.

Friedrich Nietzsche

Journaling Activities

One of the ways to enhance your experience of Wonder Walking is to write about your walks, especially when you first arrive back from your walking time. You might designate a journal specifically for writing about your walking experiences. Keep it out where you'll see it when you return so it's easy when you come back from a walk to jot down a few important insights, thoughts, feelings and new awarenesses. Your journal can serve as your own personal "Captain's Log" about your wonderful adventures and experiences of oneness.

Research has shown time and again that the simple act of expressing thoughts and feelings on paper about emotionally challenging experiences improves mental and physical health (Pennebaker, 2004).

Writing about your Wonder Walking experiences, especially regarding challenging thoughts, feelings or experiences you encountered, can promote greater health and well-being in addition to the natural benefits of walking. So be sure to take a few moments after your walks to devote to journaling as a way of supporting your health as well as creativity.

On the following pages are some different ways to journal about your Wonder Walking experiences. Try them out and see which ones spark your sense of wonder and natural creative self-expression. There's no wrong way to respond to the prompts. There are no right answers to attempt to find. The best responses are the ones that flow easily and naturally.

Allow your awarenesses and awe to flow effortlessly. Don't censor or edit what you write. Later, if you wish, you can re-read your journal writings and choose excerpts for editing, revising or expanding into poems, stories or memoir. For now, use the prompts to help enhance your walking experiences so you find greater beauty, synchronicity and wonder as you move yourself forward. Use the prompts to allow your natural healing and creative abilities to come forward more fully than they have ever before.

> *It is not what you look at that matters,*
> *it is what you see.*
>
> *Henry David Thoreau*

Reading Glasses
Left Behind

Noticing Practice I

Take a ten-minute walk outdoors in a familiar area. When you return home, complete the following prompts in your journal. You can do one or two or all of them. Complete the prompts with a word, phrase, sentence or several sentences, maybe even a paragraph or two. You can respond to each prompt once, or you can respond over and over, moving from superficial or ever-deeper self-expression, as you are sparked by what you recall from your Wonder Walks.

Duck & Cat in Harmony

Something that caught my attention .   .   .

Something I heard .   .   .

Something that soothed me .   .   .

Something I saw that left me in awe .   .   .

Something I smelled .   .   .

Something I touched .   .   .

Something that touched me physically .   .   .

Something that touched my heart .   .   .

Something that touched my spirit .   .   .

Noticing Practice II

Take a ten-minute walk in an area you haven't visited in a while or somewhere you've never taken a walk. What do you notice that's different? What do you notice that's familiar or similar?

When you return, write in your journal responses to these prompts:

Leaf Imprint in
Sidewalk Cement

Something different I noticed .   .   .

Something different I felt .   .   .

A different sound I heard .   .   .

A different scent .   .   .

I noticed new .   .   .

I noticed familiar .   .   .

I chose this new path to .   .   .

If I go this way again, I will .   .

I am proud of myself for .   .   .

Walking in this area left me
    wondering about .   .   .

Noticing Story

One Sunday morning, I spotted a small, plastic toy backhoe resting in the grass by the sidewalk. At first, I thought the bright blue and yellow colors meant I'd spotted a wrapper from a candy bar or pack of gum. I stopped to pick it up and put it in my litter bag when I noticed it was a toy. It was in perfect shape and not something to throw away. I thought to bring it home to add to my collection of interesting items from my walks and to ponder and wonder what meaning it might have for me.

As I walked a few steps with the backhoe in my hand, thinking about what I might write about my latest find, I realized the toy had belonged to someone. In fact, it still belonged to a child who might at that very moment be wondering where it happened to be.

While studying the toy's intricate design, I remembered that the evening before when I walked with my dog, I saw a young family with little boy on a tricycle walking on the sidewalk in the same area where I found the toy backhoe. I didn't know their names or where they lived although I'd seen them around the neighborhood many times.

I considered they might walk on that sidewalk again, maybe even retrace their steps to find the prized piece of tiny construction equipment. I decided not to take home my recent find.

Rather than putting the toy back in the grass where it might not be noticed by others, I placed it on top of a fire hydrant close to where I'd first spotted it in the grass. I decided to put it at eye-level for the little boy, hoping if it was his, he would recognize it when his family walked that path again. If the owner of the backhoe didn't find it, I knew someone else would find a good home for it.

I studied the toy on the fire hydrant for a moment, noticing the two man-made mechanisms that do so much to serve us. I liked the way the bright yellow cabin of the backhoe harmonized with the worn golden paint of the aged water mechanisms. Not wanting to let go totally of my experience, I photographed the special moments with my cellphone for my remembrance and wonder later on.

Remembrance Practice I

While walking today, choose something to bring home with you that you find during your walk. It can be something you like or don't like. It can be something meaningful to you right away or it can seem rather odd or even irrelevant. Trust your first hunch. If you see something and you want to pick up, and it's something available and free for you to do so, then choose to bring it home. Later, you can decide whether to keep it, throw it away, share it with someone else, or return it to where you found it.

Dove Feather

When you return from your walk, sit down and place the object in front of you. You may want to hold it in one hand while you write with the other. Then respond to these prompts in your journal. Remember to write as little or as much as comes forward, being open to moving into ever-deeper awareness of what meaning and insights this simple object may hold for you.

I found this (object) and I picked it up because .   .   .

This (object) touches my heart as or because .   .   .

This (object) inspires me by or to .   .   .

This (object) means .   .   .

I am keeping this (object) for or to .   .   .

I am discarding this (object) because .   .   .

I am recycling this (object) by .   .   .

Remembrance Practice II

Heart-shaped Leaf

While walking today, choose three items to bring home:

- o   One item for your heart
- o   One item for your mind
- o   One item for your spirit

When you return from your walk, place the objects in front of you and respond to these prompts in your journal. You may want to hold one or more objects in one hand while you write with the other hand.

I chose this (heart object) for my heart .   .   .

I chose this (mind object) for my mind .   .   .

I chose this (spirit object) for my spirit .   .   .

When I hold this (heart object), I feel .   .   .

When I hold this (mind object), I think .   .   .

When I hold this (spirit object, I sense .   .   .

This (heart object) feels .   .   .

This (mind object) reminds me .   .   .

This (spirit object) touches my soul by   .   .   .

When I look at these three objects together, I see .   .   .

When I look at these three objects together, I feel .   .   .

When I look at these three objects together, I know .   .   .

When I look at these three objects together, I think .   .   .

When I hold these three objects in my hand, I feel .   .   .

When I hold these three objects in my hand, I sense.   .   .

When I hold these three objects in my hand, I think .   .   .

*Another
Heart-shaped Leaf*

Remembrance Story

Some years ago few days after our sweet yellow Lab-mix, Buddy, passed away, I took a walk by myself. I missed Bud as he had been my good pal on daily walks for many years. He enjoyed stalking lizards, chasing squirrels, and staring down the neighborhood cats. I enjoyed his endless joy of nature and fascination with his fellow creatures.

Buddy and I had a special communication. If he wanted to go in one direction, he simply stopped and looked up at me until I got the message. If I wanted him to go in my direction and a gentle tug of his leash didn't work, then I looked into his eyes until he got the message. When he was no longer with me on our walks, I missed the way we communicated beyond words or gestures. I missed the knowing we shared as well as the joy in the small, special moments.

On that first walk without Buddy, I came across a bottle cap on the sidewalk in front of a neighbor's home. At first, I thought of how careless someone had been to simply leave a sharp bottle cap where people walk. Sometimes people walked barefoot on that sidewalk, including young children.

I picked up the rough-edged bottle cap to toss in my recycling bin. I put it in my pocket and forgot about it, feeling satisfied that I had prevented any further harm that it could do. When I got home and opened my recycling bin, ready to toss in the bottle cap, I noticed that the name on the cap was Bud Light. I stopped for a moment and wondered why this bottle cap would be named Bud Light and not the name of so many other drinks it could have been. I then I found myself smiling in that moment of wonder and awe of my own Bud's "light" that still shined for me in my heart.

I chose to keep the Bud Light bottle cap as a reminder not only of my Buddy and his sweet light but of how I can choose to see something as having a good purpose, maybe even a special message for my heart, even when at first it may appear to be annoying or in some way bad or wrong.

Since that first bottle cap, I have picked up many bottle caps as well as bottles, cups and cans. Although I choose to look for the good and the positive in whatever I pick up that could otherwise be harmful or at least annoying, those times I come across a Bud Light bottle, bottle cap or can, I smile and my heart is touched sweetly once again.

Letting Go Practice I

Hibiscus

With any of the items you've collected during your walks, you can choose to return them back to where you found them. It can be a profound and uplifting process to let go of something in this way. You can choose to make the activity memorable for you and perhaps symbolic of letting go of something you no longer need or want.

The simple practice of taking something, enjoying it for a while, receiving its meaning and message for you, and then letting it go helps us move forward with freedom. We can experience the relief that accompanies knowing we are complete and finished with something. Instead of hanging on to something we don't need any longer, putting things back and returning things to where they belong can help us make room for new experiences to come into our awareness.

Consider which of the items you've collected and are ready to return. Which one are you ready to release back to its origins? With which object have you engaged enough that you no longer need or want its presence? From which object have you learned such that you no longer need it to serve as a messenger for you?

Take the item you chose with you on your next walk.

You can return to the precise place where you found it or you might set it down somewhere that seems safe, respectful of others, and in some way meaningful to you.

You can choose to keep it rather than return it, and you can choose to decide at another time. Give yourself the freedom to let go of the object when and where it feels right. Enjoy the freedom of letting go in the way that feels freest for you.

When you return from your walk, write in your journal in response to these prompts as they fit your experience:

When I put back (object) where I found it, I felt .   .   .

When I put (object) in a different place, I felt .   .   .

When I put (object) where I found it, I noticed .   .   .

When I put (object) in a different place, I noticed .   .   .

Releasing (object) helps me remember to let go .   .   .

I decided to keep (object), and
    now I realize .   .   .

When I let go of (object), I was
    surprised by .   .   .

Holding onto (object) means .

Letting go of (object) means .

Letting of (object) allows me .

Letting Go Story

One morning as I walked into a *cul de sac* not far from my home, I noticed a large pile of household items along the street in front of someone's house. In my neighborhood, such a trash pile is picked up by the city sanitation department for free twice a year per home. When people are moving out of their homes or doing major clean-up or renovation projects, we often see a large pile such as the one I saw that day. Sometimes neighbors add their own discards to the pile, which is considered a good way to share the limited number of service calls provided by the city.

 The pile I encountered that morning included a broken wooden desk with a cracked mirror still attached to the top, a dilapidated office chair, several boxes of moldy books and vinyl record albums, and a fish tank with only three remaining glass sides. Scattered in the street in front of the trash pile were a dozen colored marbles, the kind often placed inside a fish tank or terrarium. I spotted yellow, light blue, dark blue, emerald green, and tomato-red marbles. They caught my eye as they sparkled in the morning sunlight.

I picked up the marbles, which filled my two hands, and dropped them into my shorts' pockets. They clanged and dinged together, weighing down my shorts as I walked home. Once home, I washed off the tiny glass stones, let them dry on a paper towel, and then set them in a glass bowl on my kitchen windowsill.

I noticed how light twinkled through the colors inside, and I recalled how I loved to study marbles when I was younger, wondering how what seemed to be blossoming petals appeared transfixed inside. After a few days, I moved the bowl to a book shelf, only noticing them from time to time when they happened to catch my eye.

A few weeks later, I was considering what gifts to give to two young friends of mine for their middle school graduation. As both of them were eager budding scientists, I thought to give them each a plant that they could nurture. Since Bamboo plants symbolize bringing good luck and fortune, I got them each a small stalk of Lucky Bamboo. I set each stem in a glass jar filled at the bottom with some smooth white stones from my patio. The plants looked fine but rather plain in the clear water.

I remembered the marbles. I dropped a few marbles into each container and let them settle naturally. The result was a sparkling, multi-colored foundation supporting and surrounding the sturdy green stalks --- a beautiful completion of my initial noticing, finding, and then letting go practice.

As I appreciated my creation, I saved one marble for myself in remembrance. At first I set it on my window sill, enjoying how it caught the morning sunlight. I then decided to place it on top of a bed of small pebbles surrounding a four-inch Lucky Bamboo stalk. Now, each time I look at my little plant of luck, I am reminded of my discovery and the sweet joy of letting go.

You are walking with the Lord
always in all ways
because you and the Lord are one.

John Morton

Oneness Practice

To increase your sense of the oneness of all things as you walk, here are some suggestions. During your walk, repeat this phrase to yourself silently:

I am feeling a sense of oneness with the _____.

Substitute for _____ whatever you notice in front of you or nearby --- whatever catches your attention. For example, if you're walking on a sidewalk in front of homes with trees and bushes along the way, you might say to yourself inside:

I am feeling a sense of oneness with the tall tree.

I am in oneness with the yellow flowers.

I am at one with the orange butterfly.

I am feeling at one with the leaves on the ground.

You can also simply repeat inwardly:

I am breathing in oneness with all around me.

or

I am walking in oneness with all around me.

When you return from your walk, write in your journal in response to any or all of these prompts:

I felt an experience of oneness when .　.　.

I felt an experience of oneness with .　.　.

I felt surprisingly at one with .　.　.

Noticing oneness .　.　.

Walking in oneness feels .　.　.

Walking in oneness seems .　.　.

Breathing in oneness feels .　.　.

Experiencing oneness helps me realize .　.　.

Walking in oneness helps me notice .　.　.

When I walk in oneness, I am aware .　.　.

When I walk with a sense of oneness, I feel .　.　.

Wonder Walking Practice

To enhance your sense of wonder and awe as you walk, here are some phrases to say to yourself inwardly while you are walking. As you repeat them, notice how you are feeling, thinking and experiencing your walking journey both inwardly and outwardly. You can notice how your breath changes, how your body feels at different times, and what you see and hear that leaves you with a sense of awe and  wonder. You may notice how your thoughts come and go and how your feelings change subtly or even dramatically as you walk.

Don't judge any experience as being more wondrous or awesome than another. Whether it's a small object you find, an ordinary noise, or a grand encounter that brings you to a sense of wonder, allow yourself to experience those moments of awe naturally.

Wonder can't be forced. So resist any expectations for what you might experience. There are no "shoulds" when we experience wonder. Instead, allow your natural sense of wonder and oneness to come forward in ways that are easy and gently enlightening for you.

Here are some phrases to say to yourself silently as you walk, to help experience the natural wonders of walking. In the beginning, it's easier to remember just one or two phrases. As you practice walking and saying these phrases to yourself, they will become more natural so you can vary them as you feel moved to do so.

Walking in wonder soothes me.

Walking in wonder comforts me.

Walking in wonder heals me.

Walking in wonder supports me.

Walking in wonder inspires me.

Walking in wonder clarifies my thoughts.

Walking in wonder strengthens my mind.

Walking in wonder touches my heart.

Walking in wonder nourishes my spirit.

Walking in wonder feeds my soul.

When you return from your wonder walk, write in your journal in response to these prompts:

Walking in wonder
    feels .   .   .

Walking in wonder
    seems .   .   .

Walking in wonder
    sounds .   .

When I walk in
    wonder, I know . .

When I walk in wonder,
    I notice .   .   .

Tree Frog "Waving"
from his Home
in a Lamppost

When I walk in wonder,
    I realize .   .   .

I feel a sense of wonder when .   .   .

My heart is touched by .   .   .

I now feel inspired to .   .   .

My mind is clearer, and I now know .   .   .

Wonder Walking brings .   .   .

Wonder Walking allows .   .   .

Wonder Walking seems .   .   .

Wonder Walking sounds .   .   .

Wonder Walking means .   .   .

Wonder Walking can .   .   .

Wonder Walking might .   .   .

Wonder Walking takes .   .   .

Wonder Walking makes .   .   .

Wonder Walking fulfills .   .   .

Palms at Sunset

Wonder Walking soothes .   .   .

Wonder Walking eases .   .   .

Wonder Walking shows me .   .   .

Wonder Walking seems .   .   .

Wonder Walking reminds me .   .   .

Wonder Walking is .   .   .

Ode to Wonder Walking

My mind is in wonder when I walk
Filled with tender moving thoughts

No one can tell me I am wrong
A perfect journey, short or long

Walking alone or with a friend
At the beginning or at the end

Silent communion with all around me
Butterfly, tree and bird and bee

Filled with wonder all around
Scents and textures and wealth of sound

Taking them in as I walk
Breathing in wonder and my good luck

Silent communion with engines and noise
Clamor that comes from big-time toys

Gentle movement is all it takes
Keeping my eyes and ears awake

My surroundings are full of natural sages
Listening within to wisdom of the ages

I am a blessing as I walk
Blessing even when I do not talk

Blessings reside in all I see
I bring blessings to all around me

Every day it gets better and better
Regardless of time or the weather

My mind is set for what my heart knows
Wonder Walking each day, onward I go

References

Curey, M. (2013). *Daily Rituals: How Artists Work.* New York: Knopf Doubleday.

Japanese Society of Forest Medicine (2010). *Forest Bathing. Healthy Parks Healthy People Central.* Retrieved from http://www.hphpcentral.com/article/forest-bathing.

Kuo, F. (2009). In Vindum, T. (2009), *Outdoor Fitness: Step Out of the Gym and Into the Best Shape of Your Life.* Guilford, Connecticut: Globe Pequot Press.

Nichols, S. & Watts, S. (2014). Enjoying the great outdoors – nature's own stress buster. *Economic & Social Research Council.* Retrieved from http://www.esrc.ac.uk/news-and-events/press-releases/27148/enjoying-the-great-outdoorsnatures-own-stress-buster.aspx.

Oppezzo, M. & Schwartz, D.L. (2014). Give your ideas some legs: The positive effect of walking on creative thinking. *Journal of Experimental Psychology: Learning, Memory, and Cognition, 40* (4), 1142-152.

Pennebaker, J. W. (2004). *Writing to Heal: A Guided Journal for Recovering from Trauma and Emotional Upheaval.* Oakland, California: New Harbinger Publications, Inc.

Sowden, P. (2012). Creative Walking. National Trust's Southwest Blog. Retrieved from http://www.ntsouthwest.co.uk/tag/dr-paul-sowden/

Span, P. (2011, February 8). Fitness: A Walk to Remember? Study Says Yes. *The New York Times,* D6.

References

Thompson, C., Boddy, K., Stein, K., Whear, R., Barton, J., Depledge, M.H. (2011). Does participating in physical activity in outdoor natural environments have a greater effect on physical and mental wellbeing than physical activity indoors? A systematic review. *Environmental Science Technology, 45* (5), 1761-72.

Thompson, C., Roeb, J., Aspinal, P., Mitchell, R., Clowd, A., Miller, D. (2012). More green space is linked to less stress in deprived communities: Evidence from salivary cortisol patterns. *Landscape and Urban Planning, 105* (2), 221-229.

Vindum, T. (2009). *Outdoor Fitness: Step Out Of the Gym and Into the Best Shape of Your Life.* Guilford, Connecticut: Globe Pequot Press.

About the Author

Terilee Wunderman is a
psychologist, marriage
& family therapist,
teacher, and creativity
coach with over
thirty-five years of
experience helping
children, adolescents
and adults of all ages.

Terilee utilizes art and
journal therapy
techniques to foster
healthy self-expression
and effective coping
skills for dealing with
life's challenges and
unexpected traumas.
A daily walker, Terilee
encourages appreciating
the wonder and beauty of walking outdoors to alleviate
stress and experience gratitude in our daily lives.

To learn more, please visit *www.TerileeWunderman.com.*

> *Nature does not hurry,*
> *yet everything is accomplished.*
>
> *Lao Tzu*

Take care of yourself.
Make friends with your mind and emotions.
Live in your spirit
as you walk through this day in peace.

John-Roger

12808234R10043

Made in the USA
Monee, IL
29 September 2019